The Wizard of ID
Suspended
Sentence Indeed!

Johnny Hart &
Brant Parker

CORONET BOOKS
Hodder and Stoughton

Copyright © 1976, 1977 by Field Enterprises, Inc.

First published in the United States of America in 1984
by Ballantine Books

Coronet Edition 1986

British Library C.I.P.

Hart, Johnny
  The Wizard of Id, suspended sentence indeed!
  I. Title   II. Parker, Brant
  741.5' 973   PN6727.H3/

  ISBN 0-340-38636-3

Printed and bound in Great Britain for
Hodder and Stoughton Paperbacks, a
division of Hodder and Stoughton Ltd.,
Mill Road, Dunton Green, Sevenoaks,
Kent (Editorial Office: 47 Bedford
Square, London, WC1 3DP) by
Hunt Barnard Printing Ltd.,
Aylesbury, Bucks.

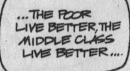

8-3

8.5

8-6

8-30

96

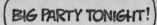

BIG PARTY TONIGHT!

I'D LIKE ONE POUND OF HAMBURGER AND SEVEN POUNDS OF CORNMEAL

9·7

GOING TO HAVE SOME CORNBALLS?

YES, BUT THEY WON'T KNOW THE DIFFERENCE

9·8

9-11

....WIZARD...IS THAT YOU?

YEAH....I'VE MADE MYSELF INVISIBLE ...PRETTY NEAT, HUH?

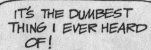

IT'S THE DUMBEST THING I EVER HEARD OF!

9-15

.... AND WIPE THAT SNEER OFF YOUR FACE!

10.6

WHERE DO THE JASPERS LIVE?

TAKE KING'S ROAD TO KING'S HIGHWAY.... GO THREE BLOCKS AND TURN LEFT ON KING'S STREET.....

...WHEN YOU COME TO KING'S BOULEVARD TAKE A LEFT...

10·7.

YES?

...IT'S THE THIRD HOVEL ON THE LEFT.

10-8

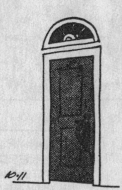

10/11

SLOG

WINE ~~TASTER~~ WANTED

10-12

10-14

10·15

10·16

11·9

11-10

ALWAYS FIGHT ON **HIGH GROUND!**

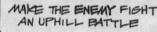

MAKE THE **ENEMY** FIGHT AN UPHILL BATTLE

...IT GIVES YOU A PSYCHOLOGICAL **EDGE**

11·18

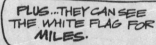

PLUS...THEY CAN SEE THE WHITE FLAG FOR **MILES.**

11·22

11·23

CAN'T YOU LEAVE YOUR WORK AT THE OFFICE?

11·26

...AND ALSO PAST PRESIDENT OF SEVERAL CLUBS AND FRATERNAL ORGANIZATIONS.

12-3

THANK YOU, SIRE.

THE DEPRESSING THING ABOUT BEING SUCCESSFUL IS THAT THEY WRITE YOUR OBITUARY SO FAR IN ADVANCE.

12-6

12-8

MY CLIENT CLAIMS YOU WATER THE WHISKEY!

HERE... TRY THIS.

DELICIOUS!... I'M DROPPING THE CASE.

12-10

HE'S HIS OWN WORST CLIENT.

I'M SORRY...WE ONLY SERVE MEN IN **THIS** ROOM.

12-11

GOOD... BRING US TWO

12-18

12·23

THERE IS AN EDITORIAL IN THE SUNDAY PAPER AGAINST DOING BUSINESS ON THE SABBATH.

ELAB

THEY'D BETTER BE CAREFUL!

1·14

WHY?

THERE WON'T BE ANY MORE SUNDAY PAPER